APRIL'S RAIN MUST FALL

APRIL'S RAIN MUST FALL

ROBERT E. MILLER

Charleston, SC
www.PalmettoPublishing.com

April's Rain Must Fall

First Edition

Paperback: 978-1-68515-139-3
eBook: 979-8-88590-083-6

*This book is dedicated to my two children,
Kristopher and Kayla, whom
I love dearly with all my heart and soul.*

TABLE OF CONTENTS

PREFACE

This book is composed of many unique poems that remind me of an artist painting a portrait where the imagery, colors, and subjects must come together simultaneously.

These poems represent who I am today and allow me to express myself emotionally. Unlike when I was growing up in Louisville, Kentucky, where parents use to say that, "a child should be seen and not heard." Over the years, I have come to realize that unless you follow your dreams, life won't be fulfilling. My son once said, "That he couldn't put his work on display for the world to see," as I am doing. Right now, I believe in taking risks and being the best version of myself.

Honestly, some of the poems in this book will help people to look inward and become the person they're meant to be, regardless of what others say. You only have one life to live, as I do, so why not live it without stop signs?

CHAPTER 1

LIFE'S BEAUTY

ROADS NEVER TRAVELED

I traveled a road of unfamiliar dreams.
There I observed separate realities,
On roads of what was and will never be.
They both echoed fears I couldn't cure.
Of twisted thoughts that have no end,
That oversees a field of broken dreams.
Disguised amid two roads, never seen
Where one road ends and another begins
That turned everything upside down.
On two roads, I've never known before.
Both challenge a life I've come to love.
Fulfilling dreams, I wouldn't have known.

STAGGERED OFF

You stagger off your feet swaying
back and forth without any relief.
Everywhere you turn you hear
music playing in the air.
Then lean side to side as you stand
staggering off with weary eyes.

Where you give yourself applause
for the motion, you longer recall.
In the myth of muddled
thoughts, you raise your
hand to invisible fans.
With every ghostly thought,
you stagger off.

In a pail of pitiless shame,
you try to reclaim your name.
By opening a gateway of doors
where you stagger off to find a new one.
On a side rail from hell,
you catch a nasty smell.

At the end of it all, you finally
find a place to catch your breath.
And raise your head high
and wave goodbye to the misery
that has always occupied your life.

PRODIGIES RISE

Sweet word's sung in a lullaby
May bring tears to your eyes.
In mesmerizing lyrics
That carry messages across time.
In a wavering tone of melodies
and jazzed-up musical lines.
Giving rise to geniuses,
No longer trapped in the dark
As the brilliance of their talent rises.
Fulfilling a destiny sought.
Of wondrous sounds of music
Cultivates their minds,
And releasing years of frustration,
where their musical notoriety arises.

THERAPY'S HEART

I listened to your burdens,
and I feel your pain.
I'm not a priest to confess your mistakes.
But my heart is wide open, and not completely closed.
I listen to complaints that only God can solve.
Do you ask why I am like this?
Yet you have asked nobody else, I bet.
Therefore, *Webster's Dictionary,* it's the book
you need to read.
That could define the frustration that's running
rampant in your head.
Of words that might give real meaning to life,
Even one's attempt to tear you down.
Be like Freud, and analyze your mind.
Look deep inside for the damage done.
Now, stop bringing me your dislike of yourself.
Life isn't what you think;
It's what you make of it.
Not a fairy-tale story with a sweet ending,
But a life of heartbreaks, setbacks, and rewards.
It's nothing you haven't heard of before.
So, the times you confess to me, your shame of yourself.
Think about the people who would like to live your life.

ENDURING REALITY

Say if my heart could cross the world
With a harvest of icy soil
Fertilizing a land of frozen snow,
With chilling thoughts that won't let go,
And finding coldness in despair.
In erroneous visions lurking in my head.
Offering a wealth of worldly thoughts
Ever-changing directions without any recourse,
Loon's a festering and cold heart,
Frozen, but warm to the touch,
Enduring a lifestyle that offers much.

LIFE TO LIVE

This is your life to live.
In a time when lies are disguised
as the truth.
Where people tend to satisfy other's desires,
And let people take away their power.
Keeping themselves infertile of mind,
Believing whatever the majority decides.
But as reality stands, the individuals with
the strongest of minds are shepherds,
and the weakest are lambs.

SOCIAL NORMS

People associate norms with social beliefs.
Ignoring the truth that we're all different in personality
Standards that want to control your mind.
Dictated by beliefs don't have any reality.
Norms that alienate people on what the majority decides.
With historical values that are fueled
by ignorance and lies.
Norms that reflect
of social myths,
stereotypes, and false
beliefs. Optical illusions
created by the powers, to
distort the truth. Pitting the
poor, against the middle class and
ethnic groups. Norms that were constructed
to keep you asleep. Wanting you to conform
to unspoken rules without resistance. Institutional
brainwashing as you can see. Depending on the weakness
of people to maintain the deceit. Norms that seek to cultivate the
minds of unwatered seeds, expecting your loyalty for them to succeed.

CREATIVE DREAMS

Life is a series of dreams.
Not amplified when we're asleep,
Unknowingly they may hold the keys to our fate.
Of creative thoughts that power the mind.
That is never-ending and
Never bending,
When dreams become difficult to define,
Our creativity will continue to thrive.
To open doors to emancipate ourselves.

BODY AND SOUL

She labored with her body
if she had an empty soul.
Her body was an open invitation.
Just like a steamship burning coal.
She was offered endless opportunities.
But she refused to betray herself.
Thus forget about the morals she was taught.
Now with an ambitious mind,
and no longer lingering in shame.
A lost soul finding purpose, now living
a life of integrity.

LIFE IS!

Life never remains the same.
When we go through things, we can't explain.
It goes by quickly before you know,
Then makes strange detours you can't ignore.
And doesn't apologize for the trouble it caused.

LEGACY TREE

Just like a twisted vine wraps itself around a tree.
The roots of our lives have a long life expectancy.
By the future that was set before we were born.
In life as we honor those who came before.
Thus, we celebrate their lifetime of accomplishments.
Where their legacy becomes a map for what we aim to achieve.
So we can travel down a path to create our destiny.
At a time, that'll require us to depend on our mentality.

THE TIP OF THE ICEBERG

You poke fun at me!
It's not an illusion in my mind.
I've schooled bigger fish without trying.
Does my intelligence disturb you?
It's only a little I show of myself.
Knowing your love for me isn't
what I thought.

You cut your eyes at me, do I care?
I'm just like a bear in the woods.
That's only dangerous when I'm threatened.

Fortunately, I feel love for the world,
but it doesn't love me back.
Like preachers writing their sermons to God.
I write my sermon to those foolish hearts.
Not angry words, as most of you might think.
But rational words that leap off the page.
Where I have respect for people who treat me right.
And feel unsettled when others try to tear me down.

They're like zombies walking around
and always wanting blood,
zombies afraid,
zombies on parade,
zombies with no conscience
and zombies dead.

15

You roll your eyes at me;
sass me with your mouth.
Talk behind my back!
Is that all you got?
I'm an eagle flying free.
With a destiny only to be
determined by me.

FRAGMENTED THOUGHTS

For every moment we treasure in our lives.
Our drive to survive will sound off like an alarm.

Like a rock that's thrown across a pond.
The rippling effects of the rock won't ever be known.

Like an artist painting a memorable masterpiece.
The mastery of the work may intrigue dreamers.

Like a poem written with eloquent words to be read.
The magic of each word will stand out like a pyramid.

Like a clock orbiting in outer space.
The rotation of its hands could cross the universe.

Like an innocent child waiting to be born.
The day of its birth shall be a blessing to all.

UNSOLVED MYSTERY

Rekindled memories lay hidden in the dark.
Memories that lay a foundation of reflected thoughts.

Of shadows of unspoken dreams that live within our minds.
That lay way across meadows of mysteries unsolved.

While incomplete, images lay stranded in broken thoughts.
Making you wonder if memories have memories of themselves.

MORNING TILL NIGHT

I'm a ringing sound that gets you up on time,
And the soft cloth that wipes your weary face.
I'm the reflection in the mirror that you look to embrace.
The brush that works to erase that unpleasant taste,
Those threads of fabric you wear every day.
The soles of rubber that take you everywhere,
And the motivation in your eyes that pushes you to survive.
And the echoes of success that give you peace at night.

DELUDED BELIEFS

We're only safe, on days we're alive.
A crazy thought that leaps out of our minds.
Twisted beliefs that make little sense
An imaginative myth to open our eyes
Deluded words that can't calculate a life
A benchmark of insanity leaves you in doubt.
Of mysterious ideas that hypnotize themselves.
With unusual thoughts that have no investors.
Witty, witty words!
Eye-popping thoughts!
That we're only safe on days we're alive,
And only alive when we see another sunrise.

CHAPTER 2
NATURE TALKS

APRIL'S RAIN

Every April, rain falls from the sky.
Each raindrop may hold the future of an innocent child.
For every season, that the rain does come,
it helps cleanse the air and fertilize the land.
Where every flower blossoms, leaves turn green,
and the sunsets above the trees.
Like every animal, a plant big or small needs rain as it falls.
In a world that's being reshaped by tropical storms
and ice melting away in the coldest of lands.
By humankind burning fossil fuels, cutting down protected trees,
polluting the air, oceans, and seas.
What will humanity do when trees no longer bear fruit,
and animal life is extinct and the air
is no longer fit to breathe?
April rain may fall from the sky; seasons will come and go,
but the human species might not be around to terrorize
the planet anymore.

WING IT, BIRDS

The songs of birds sing no lullaby of mine.
Their wings flap to a rhythm of time,
Against the brisk winds of cumulus clouds.
Birds that leave no trail of themselves behind,
And fly amid the ranges of mountaintops,
Only stopping whenever they get tired.
Graceful birds preserve the gift of flight.
Small titans with wings touching the sun's light.
Instinctively, they climb up into a celestial sky,
And overtake gravity without a compass to guide.
Species of birds flew before humans gained sight, with
painted brilliant colors, easily identified.

A RIVER OF TREES

Rivers of trees stand in a cool summer breeze.
Where tree leaves spread themselves out like eagles in flight
and bathe endlessly in the sunlight.
As every tree aspires to touch the sky to extend a branch
for a bird needing to rest.
A river of trees that have survived for a generation of time.
Where each tree drops its seeds for another one to succeed.
In a cycle of life before a man walked on land.
The rivers of trees shall continue to grow for eternity.

STANDING TALL

They stand above the rest.
In a height race that's no longer a contest.
Despite the nice view without
wearing high-heel shoes.
They stare down at your faces,
although the clouds do get in their way,
and they notice every fiber of hair,
even the wigs you may wear.
And observe the fear on your face,
as they stand above you daily.
Where most people stand below their waist,
making it harder for them to communicate.
And unable to recognize the success they achieved
wasn't because of their height, but the gifts
God gave them.

A WINTER BREEZE

Snow-covered trees stand firmly in a breeze.
While the sun hides behind the backdrop of a bluish sky,
Overlooking mountaintops that stand side by side.
And icy water flows through the uneven paths of rocks,
Beside the snow-covered trees that aren't able to stand up.
Whilst blades of icy grass reflect their shadows to selves,
And animals scurry about, waiting for winter to stop.
As the wind withers, as winter gives way to spring, as birds sing.
Where buds on trees and blades of grass show themselves
And the sunlight touches them as winter passes.

FREEDOM RUN

When sheep break free to escape their fate,
And wander across lands that capture their imaginations.
Without a pack of wolves that would chase them down.
Since nature has given them the ability to survive.
That occupies the minds of sheep every minute in time.
On a path where they seek a destiny to be found
As they run along a river that runs for miles and miles.
Only able to cross when the water is shallow.
And every sheep reaches dry land followed behind the other.
In a land where the grass is green and the air is clean.
And every sheep huddles around the other in disbelief.
That they finally found a new land they can live in peace.

RIVER SHORE

Old tree branches lay dormant on a river shore.
Each one scattered like a tapestry on a floor.
As river tides cascade back and forth.
And cinders of rocks lie even on a path.
While clouds hang in silence, searching for a storm.
And salmon leap high like acrobats on dry land.
And honeybees feed on the nectar of morning glories.
While geese fly evenly, going against the breeze.
And foxes gulp water at the river shore.
In the evening, as the sun goes down.
And blankets of light fade behind the horizon.
Even the stars dance at night without interruptions.

VASTNESS

Stars waver along an endless path
Amid the variants of brightness.
Igniting the heavens of starry light,
As if candles were covering the horizon.
And shadows of planets had crossed
distant stars.
Eclipsing moons before humans cried.
There shines a light for civilization to thrive
On a new planet that's suitable for life.
Among the billions of stars in the universe,
And give humanity a chance to survive,
Without the threat of self-destruction
and crime.

TASTY NUTS

Acorns don't climb down
out of oak trees.
Nor do they bask in the sun
without leaves.
Tasty nuts that drop
to the ground.
Unshaken by the effects
of gravity's power.
Acorns attract squirrels that
nibble, nibble, and bite their shells.
Bittersweet nuts that lie under trees
Nutty nuts of acorns, yummy to eat,
Edible, tasty nuts were plentiful for the season.

CHAPTER 3
ROMANTIC TIES

GOOSE BUMPS

My body burns as if it were on fire.
I can't believe I'm feeling this way.
Can I touch you, or should I just wait?
Knowing you're the love I think about.
Do you feel the calmness in my heart?
Or sense the storm building in our minds,
When your body touches mine
It feels like shooting stars at night.
Each one gives me goose bumps.
Every time our lips become intertwined.
Its undeniable feelings of emotions I can't deny.
Unforgettable pleasures where my body shouts.

SHAKEN EMOTIONS

I crave lost love that broke my heart.
Misfortune of emotions I couldn't abort,
Of love, no longer finding comfort in my arms.
Abandoned feelings now drifting in what was.
Shaken by the absence of passionate love
Estranged to a hollow heartbroken apart
Bittersweet emotions now thriving to be felt
Of leftover memories when you took my hand.
You cradled my body as if I was your last.
Uncensored touches that kept me aroused.
And the pleasure I felt when we kissed on the couch.
Now a long-forgotten love I can only think about.
A beautiful romance, that took my breath away.

PRECIOUS LOVE

You're the vision that drives my every thought.
I'll be that prayer you hold in your heart.
You'll be the breeze that lifts my wings high.
I'll be that fire burning in your eyes.
You'll be that distinguished love lying within my reach.
I'll be that lost lover no longer drifting out at sea.
You'll be that precious pearl lying in the deep.
I'll be that gemstone for you to keep.
You'll be that eternal light within my sight.
I'll be the one who holds your heart at night.

OPEN YOUR HEART

Open up your heart to explore the hidden beauty inside.
Forget the past, as time erases what doesn't last.
Open up your heart for the sun to shine in.
Don't hold on to mental pain that may drain you.
Open up your heart for love's gentle touch.
Remember the mistakes of the past without any regrets.
Open up your heart like a ship charting a new course.
And anchor your heart in waters where your feet touch.

SENSUAL PLEASURES

I whisper in your ear.
You taste the spice in my mouth.
Our feet touch at the edge.
As our pillows slide off the bed,
I smell a perfume odor.
Something sensual comes to mind.
We hold each other's hands.
Once the candles begin to die,
Our souls kiss the other.
Bringing euphoria to our eyes of
pleasures beyond measure
that won't ever die.

FIELDS OF LILIES

Your love is mine, and it's true.
Among the fields of lilies, it passes through.
Each day the clouds may fade away,
But your love is unconditional.
Like a lily that sits on a mountaintop.
It captures the beauty in your heart.
With an unforgettable scent that opens my eyes.
Of passionate love, that's truly ours.

WILDFIRE

Love is a deep feeling in the heart.
An addictive sensation that spreads like wildfire.
It burns more intensely as a relationship grows.
Engulfs you in flames to open up your eyes,
Evokes every feeling in your body and mind.
Of uncontrollable love that fulfills your desires.
Awakening you to emotions you can't ignore.
Of feelings of affection you can't control.
That can't be extinguished once the flames go out.

INFECTIOUS DREAMS

You're the mystery in my dreams.
The light shines even at night.
The angle in my heart I can't figure out.
An infectious love where I need life support.
A pragmatic dream festers inside me.

CROSSING LOVE'S BRIDGE

One bridge crossed over too many times.
Whereabouts fantasy seeks reality in love.
That no doctor's diagnosis can resolve.
When love grows to measure the affection of
tears flowing,
bodies tasting,
and lips clinging.
Stirring up emotions we're powerless to control.
Whereby love becomes the architect of the mind,
Of physical sensations, we can't deny.
On a bridge that goes one way
with no detours to place love in danger.

BROKEN HEART

I drove with love, and it didn't make a peep, as
It rested itself quietly on my seat.
You wouldn't believe how Love made me feel, as
We drove around town in an Oldsmobile.
Then, one day, as Love and I were driving along,
Love told me it was moving on.
Well, I couldn't get Love off my mind.
While I wiped the tears running down my eyes,
And stared into Love's unresponsive face,
When it opened its door and walked away.

CHAPTER 4

45

CULTURALLY FAVORED

THEY RISE

PREJUDICE

UNDER A SOCIETAL WHIP

SKIN COLORS

REEFS OF CULTURAL BELIEFS

NOT FREE YET

TOLERANCE

THEY RISE

Yes, O God, our ancestors had colorful dreams.
Slaves were chained beyond the sea.
Tortured for centuries to destroy their humility
Born to ancestors who stood among kings
Who flourished along
the shores of coastal seas.
Those descendants of the Garden of Eden
Generation after generation,
they sought their place.
Beyond the boundaries of reality
Brave souls with memories of the past
Who came forth to claim their prize.
Self-determined prodigies
drifting against the tide
Daydreamers
with the willingness to thrive.
Infused with courage
since the beginning of time.
Yes, they rise to claim their prize.
Those scholars, inventors,
and trailblazers;
Free spirits staring at their fate,
leaving no path unchallenged.
Yes, they rise;
they rise to claim their prize.
Students of life's struggles
filled with creativity.
Educated minds,

no longer chained to pain and suffering.
Yes, they rise;
they rise to claim their prize.

PREJUDICE

Prejudice is like weeds, hard to get rid of
despite what society has achieved.
We try to educate people in all kinds of
ways, but prejudice is hard to eliminate.
They teach it in our homes, books, and
streets. No wonder why people have found
no relief.
People build walls of endless deceit to
maintain their mindless disease.
They spread their stereotypes like a rash of
hate, fearing one day their ideas might
dissipate.
As they prey on the innocence of the human
race, spreading their hatred to others
around.
In the gratitude of respect, people should
reject the prejudice that lies deep within their
minds and what tries to generalize.
And only accept that prejudice exists
because of primitive fears and personal
ignorance.

UNDER A SOCIETAL WHIP

No matter where minorities may turn,
The oppression of the past will always remain.
Oppressors would wholeheartedly disagree, saying,
That freedom does exist for those who aren't on a vetting list.
But, as realistic as it stands, the oppressed would not complain
if the rights of the oppressor were equally the same.
Until society opens its eyes to that prejudice, injustice
And its deceit is a social disease,
The illusion that freedom exists will always
remain under a societal whip.

SKIN COLORS

We weaponize the colors
of people's skin because of ignorance
and fear.
Normalizing false beliefs
that challenge God's will.
The cynicism of lies that
ignore the reality of the truth.
Indoctrinated by angry cowards
who can't face themselves.
Using people's skin colors
like a natural resource to destroy.
Unearthing the seeds of bitterness
that fuel emotional hate.
That allows prejudice to grow,
as if a monster on steroids.
Tearing through the feeble minds
of people out of control.
That generates centuries of unneeded
mental pain and anxiety.
Needing another destination
For a new generational change.
But just not a history lesson
of thoughtless grandiosity.
Preserving humanity to the need
of reconciliation and peace.
Not impeded by the weapon
of skin colors that divide people.

REEFS OF CULTURAL BELIEFS

Every nation is a beautiful coral reef under
the sea.
Where people's beliefs are embedded in their reef
and passed down for centuries.
These beliefs were socially accepted by
the people of the time.
Where their beliefs gave rise to strong families,
communities, and cultural ties.
And those values were socially instilled
in every woman, man, and child.
In a sea of reefs where people have
the right to practice
their cultural beliefs, religion,
and be treated equally.
And live a life of prosperity.

NOT FREE YET

I was born into bondage.
Of course, I have scars on my back.
And I had no idea what emancipation meant.
For years, I lived a life in hellish pain.
When night came and went,
it was never the same.
And I remember friends got caught trying to escape.
I could hear the whips cracking and rattling chains.
My body just cringed, not to suffer the same.
Yes, freedom did come but came at a cost.
Their ex-owners sought servitude with papers attached.
And the old master says I can sharecrop to have my own.
Shall I accept the offer or just move on?
Notwithstanding the abuse of the past;
Now faced with hatred, sprung up overnight.
What can free slaves do to protect themselves?
Of segregated laws designed to strangle their rights.
While night riders want to torture free slaves to death.
Was this the actual emancipation Lincoln meant?

TOLERANCE

We all live on planet earth,
where we share the same resources every day.
Despite the barriers that exist in our social beliefs.
People must work together to resolve
the world's hostility, regardless of our state of mind.
We need to challenge ourselves
and learn to accept others' cultural beliefs,
to establish a world with justice and peace.

CHAPTER 5

55

EXCLUSIVELY DESIGNED

MASTERFUL POET

PORTRAIT NAMED

ORANGE PLATYPUS

OVAL SHAPES

MASTERFUL POET

A poem doesn't describe the poet,
Nor the genius behind the craft
Who is a skillful and artistic person.
Whose talents may take your breath away.
With creative words that illuminate themselves.
Through original phrases to unravel your mind
Lively sentences to set your heart on fire,
And meaningful rhymes that speak out loud.

PORTRAIT NAMED

A picture on the wall cannot describe its frame.
While Whistler's mother sat motionless in a chair.
Wearing a bonnet loosely fitted,
and clothes worn as if of a handkerchief.
The room's long drapes rested to resist the light.
And her rosy cheeks, nose, and eyes stood out.
Giving the artist ingenious strokes of imagery design.
An extraordinary tone of colors that was explicitly profound.

ORANGE PLATYPUS

Platypus sat on his tush.
With bushy, wide eyes in his thoughtful thoughts.
Saddened because he had lost his mate.
Tears were running unevenly down his face.
Then Platypus told his troubles to a mouse.
Whose ears burned like a forest on fire.
And then he gave Platypus some simple advice.
Vigorously shaken by what he just heard.
Platypus turned aside and laughed at himself.
Unwittingly surprised that he was
talking to a mouse.

OVAL SHAPES

The drawings on the wall aren't mine.
Some with long-shaped ovals as a Picasso painting
Each one had a mixture of colors saturated in blue.
Brilliantly preserved as if they were heirlooms
One so oddly shaped, similar to a willow leaf.
Others intricately aligned, like a Rubik's Cube.
An array of subtle colors in a masterpiece
Undefined textures that distract the eye
Visible shapes that affect the mind
Of radiated colors splattered on the wall.
Long oval shapes were a mystery to all.

APPRECIATION

Thanks for taking the time to read this book and rate it.

ABOUT THE AUTHOR

Robert is an author, writer, and poet. He grew up in Louisville, Kentucky, and is a notable alumnus of Louisville Central High School, which legendary boxing champion Muhammad Ali also attended. He graduated from the University of Cincinnati, where he played collegiate basketball, and afterward he played professionally. Robert was an inductee in both his high school and college athletic halls of fame. At present, Robert lives in Cincinnati, Ohio, and has two children, Kristopher and Kayla.